WHAT IF You Need to Call 911?

by Anara Guard

illustrated by Mike Laughead

PICTURE WINDOW BOOKS
a capstone imprint

Thanks to our adviser for his expertise and advice:
Terry Flaherty, PhD
Professor of English
Minnesota State University, Mankato

Editor: Shelly Lyons
Designer: Ashlee Suker
Art Director: Nathan Gassman
Production Specialist: Sarah Bennett
The illustrations in this book were created digitally.

Picture Window Books
151 Good Counsel Drive
P.O. Box 669
Mankato, MN 56002-0669
877-845-8392
www.capstonepub.com

All books published by Picture Window Books
are manufactured with paper containing at least
10 percent post-consumer waste.

Library of Congress Cataloging-in-Publication Data
Guard, Anara.
 What if you need to call 911? / by Anara Guard.
   p. cm. — (Danger zone)
 Includes index.
 ISBN 978-1-4048-6682-9 (library binding)
 ISBN 978-1-4048-7037-6 (paperback)
 1. Assistance in emergencies—Juvenile literature.
 2. Telephone—Emergency reporting systems—Juvenile literature.
 3. Emergencies—Juvenile literature. 4. Safety education—Juvenile
literature. I. Title. II. Series.
 HQ770.7.G83 2012
 613.6083—dc22   2011006550

Printed in the United States of America in North Mankato, Minnesota.
032011   006110CGF11

An emergency is when someone needs help fast. In an emergency, an adult calls 911 for help. But what if you have an emergency when an adult isn't there?

The stories in this book will help you know when to call 911 and what to say. Follow the safety tips to get help from rescue workers quickly.

What If Someone Is Really Sick?

Jacob's grandfather is very sick and won't wake up. No one else is home, so Jacob calls 911. A dispatcher answers.

Jacob takes a deep breath and answers all of her questions

SAFETY TIP

Stay calm! Speak slowly so the dispatcher can understand you.

What If Someone Gets Hurt?

Carla and Mike are home alone. Mike tries climbing the tree in the yard. He falls and hurts his leg. He can't move it.

Carla runs inside and calls 911.

**Dispatcher:** Put down the phone and go unlock the gate or door. Then rescue workers will be able to get to Mike.

SAFETY TIP
Listen up! Follow the dispatcher's instructions so rescue workers can get to you.

What If You Don't Know Where You Are?

Jackson calls 911 when he sees a car accident.

Dispatcher: Where are you? Can you read the street signs?

SAFETY TIP

Look around! When outdoors, find street signs or large buildings with signs. These things will help rescuers find you.

Jackson reads the signs out loud.
The rescue workers arrive quickly.

What If You Can't Think of the Words?

After school, Tony jumps off the swing and hits his head. Ella uses her phone to call 911.

Dispatcher: Where is he?

Ella is scared. She points at Tony and says, "He's right there!"

14

On the playground at Brewster Public School.

Dispatcher: I'm sending help right away.

SAFETY TIP

Be clear! When answering a dispatcher, use details. The clearer you are, the quicker help will arrive.

15

What If You See a Crime?

Justin sees someone trying to break into a car. He calls 911 and tells the dispatcher. The dispatcher says not to go near the car.

SAFETY TIP

Be safe! If you see a crime or are in an emergency, go where you will be safe. Then call 911.

What If You See a Fire?

Lila calls 911 when she sees a fire. She answers all of the dispatcher's questions.

He tells her to stay on the phone. Soon she hears sirens. The fire engines are on their way!

SAFETY TIP

Don't hang up! Stay on the phone until the dispatcher tells you to hang up.

What If I Call by Mistake?

Anna thinks the cell phone is turned off, so she practices dialing 911.

The dispatcher answers! She doesn't send fire engines or police cars. She tells Anna it is good to practice, but to do it with a grown-up.

SAFETY TIP

Practice calling 911 with an adult. But don't really call unless you need help for an emergency.

Dialing 911 in an emergency can be scary. If you follow these tips, a dispatcher will send help quickly:

- ◉ Stay calm! Speak slowly, so the dispatcher can understand you.

- ◉ Listen up! Follow the dispatcher's instructions, so rescue workers can find you.

- ◉ Look around! When outdoors, look around for street signs. The street names will help rescuers find you.

- ◉ Be clear! When answering a dispatcher, use specific details.

- ◉ Be safe! If you see a crime or are in an emergency, go where you will be safe. Then call 911.

- ◉ Don't hang up! Stay on the phone until the dispatcher tells you to hang up.

- ◉ Practice calling 911 with an adult. If you call 911 by accident, tell the dispatcher it was a mistake.

Spot the Emergencies!

Which two pictures show emergencies?

GLOSSARY

crime—an action that is against the law

detail—an important fact or information

dispatcher—a person who answers 911 calls and sends help

emergency—when someone needs help fast

rescue worker—a person who arrives at an emergency in an ambulance, police car, or fire truck

MORE BOOKS TO READ

Denshire, Jayne. *Safety.* Healthy Habits. Mankato, Minn.: Smart Apple Media, 2011.

Johnson, Jinny. *Being Safe.* Now We Know About. New York: Crabtree Pub. Company, 2010.

Waxman, Laura Hamilton. *Ambulances on the Move.* Lightning Bolt Books: Vroom-Vroom. Minneapolis: Lerner Publications Co., 2011.

INTERNET SITES

FactHound offers a safe, fun way to find Internet sites related to this book. All of the sites on FactHound have been researched by our staff.

Here's all you do:

Visit *www.facthound.com*

Type in this code: 9781404866829

Super-cool stuff! Check out projects, games and lots more at **www.capstonekids.com**

ABOUT THE AUTHOR

Anara Guard is a short story writer and poet who has worked in the field of injury prevention since 1993. She speaks around the country on a variety of topics related to unintentional and intentional injury. For seven years, she worked for the Children's Safety Network, a national injury and violence prevention resource center. Ms. Guard has also been a parent educator and a librarian. She has a master's degree in library and information science and a certificate in maternal and child health. The mother of two grown sons, she lives and writes in California.

INDEX

answering questions, 6–7, 13–15, 18

car accidents, 10
crimes, 16

dispatchers, 4, 5, 6, 9, 10, 13, 15, 16, 18, 19, 20, 21

fires, 18
following instructions, 9, 21
forgetting the words, 13–15

going to a safe place, 17, 21

injuries, 8, 12

practicing calling 911, 20, 21

reading street signs, 11, 21
rescue workers, 3, 9, 11, 21

sicknesses, 4
staying calm, 7, 21
staying on the phone, 19, 21

using details, 15, 21